R. L. STINE

Titles in the *Authors Teens Love* series:

Ray Bradbury
Master of Science Fiction and Fantasy
0-7660-2240-4

Joan Lowery Nixon
Masterful Mystery Writer
0-7660-2194-7

R. L. Stine
Creator of Creepy and Spooky Stories
0-7660-2445-8

J. R. R. Tolkien
Master of Imaginary Worlds
0-7660-2246-3

E. B. White
Spinner of Webs and Tales
0-7660-2350-8

AUTHORS TEENS LOVE

R. L. STINE

Creator of Creepy and Spooky Stories

Michelle Parker-Rock

Enslow Publishers, Inc.

40 Industrial Road   PO Box 38
Box 398   Aldershot
Berkeley Heights, NJ 07922   Hants GU12 6BP
USA   UK

http://www.enslow.com

Library of Congress Cataloging-in-Publication Data

Parker-Rock, Michelle.
    R.L. Stine : creator of creepy and spooky stories / Michelle Parker-
Rock.— 1st ed.
        p. cm. — (Authors teens love)
    Includes bibliographical references and index.
    ISBN 0-7660-2445-8
    1. Stine, R. L.—Juvenile literature. 2. Young adult fiction—
Authorship—Juvenile literature. 3. Authors, American—20th century—
Biography—Juvenile literature. 4. Horror tales—Authorship—Juvenile
literature. I. Title. II. Series.
PS3569.T4837Z84   2005
813'.54—dc22

                                    2005004234

Printed in the United States of America

10 9 8 7 6 5 4 3 2 1

To Our Readers: We have done our best to make sure all Internet Addresses
in this book were active and appropriate when we went to press. However,
the author and publisher have no control over and assume no liability for
the material available on those Internet sites or on other Web sites they may
link to. Any comments or suggestions can be sent by e-mail to
comments@enslow.com or to the address on the back cover.

Cover Illustration: Courtesy of R. L. Stine (foreground); Erin Polke
(background).

Photos and Illustrations: All photos courtesy of R. L. Stine, except
pp. 9, 59, 66, courtesy of Michelle Parker-Rock.

CONTENTS

For my brother, Harvey,
who always enjoys a good story.

MPR

CHAPTER 1

WHO IS R. L. STINE?

When asked if he would do an interview for this book, R. L. Stine replied, "I'm so flattered that you want to write about me! Thank you so much."[1] These are humble words for a person who is one of the most popular authors of books for middle grade readers and young teens. Stine's modest response reflects his humility. Stine's sales of more than three hundred million books is a testimony to his success.[2]

R. L. Stine's renowned writing career began in 1986, at the age of forty-three, when he accepted an offer to write a frightening story for teens.[3] That first scary novel, *Blind Date*, took off like gangbusters, and it immediately topped the young adult best-seller charts.[4] He went on to write *Fear Street*, a series of horror novels for readers aged nine to fourteen.[5]

The *Fear Street* stories were embraced by horror-genre-loving kids, and Stine immediately saw a niche for himself as a writer. With *Fear Street* paving the way, Stine began to work on a new series called *Goosebumps*. The *Goosebumps* stories were aimed at a younger audience.[6] Stine made the stories creepy, but he also made them funny. *Goosebumps* was such a huge triumph with readers aged eight to twelve that it became one of the most popular hit book series of all time.[7]

All over the country, in homes with school-aged children, Stine's name became a household word. From 1994–1996, he was recognized by *USA Today* as the number-one best-selling author in America.[8] The *Guinness World Records Millennium Edition 2000* lists Stine's *Goosebumps* as the world's top-selling children's book series.[9] To date, more than two hundred million *Goosebumps* books have been published. The books have been translated into sixteen languages in thirty-one nations and have achieved best-seller status in Germany, Italy, Spain, Australia, and other places around the world.[10] There is no doubt that *Goosebumps* is a global sensation and that R. L. Stine is an international celebrity.

Stine's superstar presence goes well beyond the book industry. His name is associated with a wide range of mass media projects and merchandised products. In 1995, *Goosebumps* was made into a series of regularly broadcast TV programs that were popular in both the United States and Canada. *Goosebumps* also aired as afterschool specials.[11] Fans could buy home videos which sold more than a million copies, as well as scary T-shirts, hats, games, puzzles, and other paraphernalia to quench their *Goosebumps* mania. A *Goosebumps* board game by Milton Bradley sold well as did a card game by Parker Brothers.

The books of author R. L. Stine (above) have sold over 300 million copies altogether.

Goosebumps also made its way to Disney-MGM Studios in Florida, where visitors could have a spooky experience with characters from the series. Stine's creations appear at the theme park's Horrorland Fright Show and Fun House and star some of the scariest *Goosebumps* characters.

Audiences can see another one of Stine's footprints in several other major theme parks, including Busch Gardens. *The Haunted Lighthouse* is a 4-D adventure movie attraction based on an original story written by Stine. The film combines state-of-the-art visuals with multisensory special effects.

Until 1995, Stine wrote only juvenile fiction. Eager to reach still another readership, Stine tried his hand at writing horror for grown-ups. He received a million-dollar advance to write a thriller for adults.[12] The book, *Superstitious*, was published by Warner Books. It received mixed reviews but generally sold well.[13]

It was not until 2003 that Stine tried his hand at writing another adult novel, *The Sitter*, published by Ballantine Books. Then, a year later, Ballantine Books released Stine's third adult title, *Eye Candy*. While Stine's books for adults demonstrated his wide-ranging ability to entertain, his endless efforts to give young audiences quick scary thrills propelled his celebrated success.

In 2001, Stine launched yet another children's series, *The Nightmare Room*. This series offered readers both books and an innovative, interactive online website. That same year, *The Nightmare Room* television show was broadcast on the Kids' WB network. In conjunction with Parachute Publishing and HarperCollins Publishers, Stine also created "*The Nightmare Room* Writing Program," a free

Stine proudly displays the cover of his book, *The Haunting Hour*.

classroom writing kit that educators can download from *The Nightmare Room* website.[14]

The list of credits for this prolific, best-selling children's author goes on and on. It almost seems as if Stine was born famous, but that is not the case. Bobby Stine grew up in an older house in the poorer part of an affluent town.[15] However, he was rich in other ways.

Bobby Stine had a vivid imagination, a thirst for stories, and, above all, a passion for writing. He loved stories so much that he spent hours listening to them on the radio. He was enchanted by the fairy tales his mother read to him, and he was beguiled by the adventures of the superheroes and science fiction characters in the comic books, the magazines, and the movies that were popular during his childhood.[16]

Bobby Stine not only loved listening to stories, he also loved writing them. But as a child, he was not thinking about plots that involved bloody monsters or haunted masks. More than anything else, Bobby Stine wanted to be funny. He wanted to write comics, and he wanted to make people laugh.[17]

So how did a child with a penchant for humor turn to horror and eventually attain fame and acclaim? Who is R. L. Stine and how funny or scary is he? What is the story of the man behind the stories? It may have begun with a dare . . . or was it a scare?

Chapter 2

Dare
or Scare?

Bobby Stine had to discover the secret of the attic and time was running out. If he was ever going to find out about the monster that lurked on the top floor, he would have to do it without delay.[1]

Whatever was in the attic must be something truly awful and scary. His mother told him never to go up there. "Don't ask!" she warned him.[2] So night after night he stared up at the ceiling, boring a hole through the floorboards with his imagination. What was it? What did it look like? How truly evil was it? He had to know the truth.

In the dark and dusty off-limits chamber above his bedroom, among the trunks and the old cardboard cartons, there must be a monster so terrible that Mrs. Stine forbade her son to go there. Time after time, Bobby's mother warned him to never, ever, go into the attic. Aha! That was the catch. She told *Bobby* not to go there. She never said anything about Captain Grashus, the world's most powerful, most courageous, most unbeatable superhuman creation of Bobby himself.[3]

When Bobby found out that his father was changing jobs and that his childhood house with the big yard and the mysterious attic was up for sale, he knew that he had to act fast.[4] Captain Grashus did not have much time left.

Bobby needed a plan. He was counting on his younger brother Bill to help. Bill usually complied with Captain Grashus's commands because Bill was just a Ranger and no match for Bobby dressed in his superpowered suit. It was a Ranger's duty to do as the Captain ordered. But this time Bill refused to go along. He warned Bobby not to go, although he did agree not to tell their mother.[5]

Captain Grashus donned his bath towel cape and waited for darkness to descend. He slowly opened

---

Whatever was in the attic must be something truly awful and scary.

---

the attic door and spied the darkened stairwell. The blackness was overpowering, so he flipped on the switch, bathing the steps in just enough light to guide his passage upward.[6]

He pushed his way through cobwebs and dust, keeping his balance on the uneven attic floor. Then he stopped and looked around. What? There was nothing to see except an old garment rack where his mother had hung some of her old dresses and his dad's used work clothes. Where were the trunks and the cardboard boxes that concealed the secrets of his imaginings? How could this be the forbidden attic that he waited all this time to enter?[7]

Feeling very disappointed, Bobby turned to leave. Then suddenly, a small black dusty case caught his eye. He bent down to pick it up by its creaky handle. The lock made a sharp cracking sound when he opened the lid. What was this? A discovery! The lettering on the round black keys glistened in the glow of the attic light.

Bobby's excitement returned, and he started back down the attic stairs with an old portable typewriter under his arm.[8]

CHAPTER 3

HUMBLE BEGINNINGS

R. L. Stine is a tall man, towering over his young fans and many of his adult contemporaries. His large physical presence is accentuated by a dark complexion, jet black hair, and full bushy eyebrows. His appearance is very commanding. By contrast, this author of horror books for young people has a warm smile, dreamy eyes, and a soft-spoken voice.

When asked if people recognize him as the famous author of horror books for young readers, Stine answered, "Kids do. I hosted all those *Goosebumps* shows. I did about eight or ten *Goosebumps* shows in prime time on Fox and I hosted them all. We sold about 5 million videos that had my face on them. So I get recognized from that. I have done the *Today* show a lot. When you do a lot of television you start to get recognized.

But it's always kids. It's always the nicest kids."[1]

The timing of Bobby Stine's arrival was a surprise for his parents. They were expecting him to be born closer to Halloween, a birthday suitable for the "master of terror" that he is today. Instead, Lewis and Anne Stine welcomed their baby boy, Robert Lawrence, on October 8, 1943, several weeks before the due date.[2]

Bobby Stine was born in Columbus, Ohio. He grew up in a picturesque town called Bexley, just four miles from downtown Columbus. Bexley's tree-lined streets, Commonwealth Park, and the theater on Main Street are typical landmarks of the tranquil suburban setting where Lewis and Anne Stine raised their growing family. Bobby is the oldest of the three

---

> **"I did about eight or ten *Goosebumps* shows in prime time on Fox and I hosted them all."**
> **—R.L. Stine**

Stine children. Bill was born three years after Bobby, and Pam was born four years after Bill.[3]

At the time, Bexley was a thriving, prosperous community, but the Stines themselves were not wealthy. Bobby's grandparents had emigrated from Russia in the early 1900s. Lewis Stine, his dad, was a laborer at a restaurant supply house. Anne Stine worked equally as hard nurturing the children and making a home.[4]

The Stines lived in a small unpretentious house far from the center of town. Although their house was

A newborn Robert Stine is held by his mother, Anne.

just two blocks from the governor's mansion, it was not in the most desirable section of town. In fact, the Stines' house was just a few doors from the railroad tracks.[5]

Bobby's parents wanted to bring up their family in Bexley. They wanted Bobby, Bill, and Pam to go to good schools and to have a good life. Anne and Lewis Stine did everything they could to give their children what they needed and what they wanted.[6]

Bobby knew that his family was not as affluent as many of the other families in their town. As a teenager, he was conscious of the big cars his peers drove and of the stylish clothes his classmates wore.[7] He often felt he did not belong in such a well-to-do community.[8]

The Stines did not want their children to feel deprived. It was important to Anne and Lewis Stine that Bobby, Bill, and Pam became well-educated. They did their best to make sure that the children got all they could afford.

As an adult, Stine has no regrets about his upbringing. "I think that my feeling like an outsider as a kid helped to make me a writer," he said in his book, *It Came From Ohio! My Life as a Writer.* "I always seemed to be standing away from the crowd, watching everyone. I became an *observer,* which is part of what a writer does."[9]

The observant Bobby Stine, a boy with humble beginnings in a small Midwestern town, went on to become R. L. Stine, best-selling author and modern-day "king of horror." The young one-fingered typist put an old creaky typewriter to good use.

CHAPTER 4

THE ONE-FINGERED TYPIST

No one becomes a famous author, or a writer, for that matter, just because of a typewriter. But Stine and his first typewriter were like peanut butter and jelly, a perfect combination. He quickly discovered that he could type faster than he could write with a pencil, even if he typed with just one finger.[1] When he saw that his first little typewritten humor magazines looked much more polished than the ones he had been making by hand, he was very encouraged.

"I just started typing little magazines, joke magazines, funny stuff and little stories. I don't know why. I was a weird kid, I guess. I never went out. My parents would say, 'Go out and play. What's the matter with you?'"[2]

Nothing was the matter with Bobby Stine as long as he could do what he wanted to do. Even at the tender of age of nine, Bobby knew exactly what it was that he loved. With one finger, an old typewriter, and lots of ideas, Bobby Stine made his childhood dream come true—to write and illustrate magazines and comic books.[3]

Many ideas for Bobby's early projects, as well as for his later published work, came from his favorite form of boyhood entertainment. He was strongly influenced by the popular radio shows of the 1950s like *The Shadow* and *Suspense*. *The Shadow* featured radio's most famous mystery man who stamped out crime. *Suspense* presented plays about life-and-death situations.

Stine was inspired by the great storytelling of Jean Shepherd, the creator of the popular film, *A Christmas Story*. Shepherd's radio show was broadcast live from New York City.[4] In fact, Shepherd's funny, captivating prose about his family and his childhood piqued Bobby's interest about going to live and work in the Big Apple one day.

Stine remembers the goofy shenanigans that he and his brother Bill shared growing up. They had the usual pillow fights, but they also chattered about the stories and the characters they remembered so well from their favorite radio broadcasts and movies. But there was something else on young Bobby's mind. He was passionate about comic books and comic book heroes. Bobby could not get enough of the horror comics, published by EC, which stood for, ironically, Educational Comics.

Bobby's favorites were EC's *Tales from the Crypt* and *Vault of Horror*. He also treasured the hilarious antics in *Mad*, a humor magazine also published by EC at that time.[5] But Mrs. Stine did not approve. She called the comics and magazines trash, and she

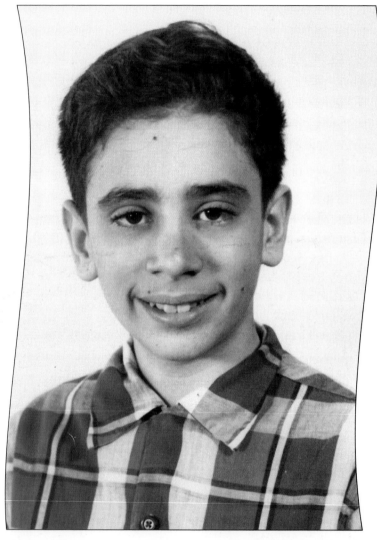

Bobby Stine greatly enjoyed reading and writing when he was growing up. Among his favorite reading material were the classic comics *Tales from the Crypt*, *Vault of Horror*, and *Mad*.

did not want her Bobby wasting his time with unworthy reading material.[6]

Bobby was a good boy, so when his mother banned the magazines from the house, he unhappily acquiesced. But it did not take long before Bobby located a place where he could get plenty of the genre he loved. Every Saturday he went down to the local barbershop where the owner kept stacks of comic books for the customers to read while they waited. Mrs. Stine often wondered why it took Bobby such a long time just to get his hair trimmed.[7] For Bobby, the arrangement worked just fine. And when he was not busy reading, he was busy writing.

Comic books had a powerful impact on young Bobby, not only as a reader, but as a writer as well. He envisioned himself drawing his own comic magazines for the rest of his life.[8] Even more than that, he wanted to create magazines and cartoons with his own original cast of satirical superhuman characters.

Bobby put his old typewriter to work. His first major effort was a tiny three-by-four-inch joke and riddle magazine called, *The All New Bob Stine Giggle Book*.[9] Bobby wrote and illustrated it. However, he soon realized that he was better at writing than he was at drawing.

When Bobby was about thirteen years old, he produced the one and only copy of *HAH! For Maniacs Only!*[10] The homemade funny book parodied the popular television shows of the day. It featured Bobby's drawings done with pens, pencils, and crayons. His next funny book was actually seven issues of *From Here to Insanity*.[11] The little magazines made fun of familiar characters of the period.

Bobby got a real kick out of showing off these creations. Bill was always a good audience. But

A thirteen-year-old Bobby Stine is shown here on the day of his bar mitzvah.

Bobby could not resist bringing the books to school and sharing them with his friends in his classes, especially if he could get some good laughs. The kids ate them up and Bobby was in seventh heaven. On the other hand, his teachers did not appreciate the disruptions and distractions that ensued. Needless to say, Stine does not recall much support from his instructors.

"Teachers tried to get me to stop. I would bring in the stuff that I wrote and I'd pass it around the room. And the teachers would say, 'Bob, please stop, please stop doing this.' So I didn't really get encouragement."[12]

Bobby held his own. He did not neglect his studies, and he was always a good student. He managed to keep his head above water where school was concerned. But what really kept Bobby going, and what really meant the world to him, was his driving ambition to be funny and to be creative.

When it came time for Bobby's bar mitzvah, the Jewish rite of passage marking his thirteenth birthday, he asked his parents for a new heavy-duty typewriter as a gift.[13] His parents were happy to grant his request. The new typewriter would make it easier and faster to fulfill his ambition, even if he had to do it with only one finger.

CHAPTER 5

SCARED OR SCARY?

It seems only natural that R. L. Stine's fans would wonder if the author was a scared child or a scary child. In *It Came From Ohio!*, Stine candidly reveals some insights.

"I was a fearful kid," he told Joe Arthur, a college pal and chronicler of Stine's early years.[1]

Stine thinks that he embraced frightening stories because he actually viewed the world as a scary place in which to grow up.[2] To make matters worse, Stine was neither athletic nor particularly brave as a young boy. He was very afraid of many things in everyday life, including even simple acts like jumping into a swimming pool, something he still will not do today.

Stine did what Stine did best. Tucked away safely in his room, he found comfort and exhilaration writing stories.

"This is the mysterious part. Why did I find it so interesting to stay in my room typing stories hour after hour? What was so interesting about that, making little comic magazines and bringing them into school? Other kids would be out playing," Stine recollected.[3]

When Bob did go out, he loved going to the movies. He and brother Bill were passionate about the low-budget movies that made them howl with fright and laughter. They went every Sunday afternoon to the local movie house where they watched classics, such as *It Came From Beneath the Sea*, *Night of the Living Dead*, and *The Creature From the Black Lagoon*.[4] The bigger the monsters were, the better the boys enjoyed the movie. They would scream at the screen when the monsters attacked. Years later, Stine remembered those movies when thinking of chilling titles for his horror novels.

> ## "This is the mysterious part. Why did I find it so interesting to stay in my room typing stories hour after hour?"
> ### —R. L. Stine

As a child, Bob was not great at sports. His skinny frame was not well-suited for the rigors of football, although he loved watching the Cleveland Browns. He was not a good shot with a basketball, so that did not work. Baseball was out because he lacked good batting skills, but he liked to see the Cleveland Indians play. Then, just when he thought he had

Robert Stine's yearbook photo.

found his game, bowling, he broke his toe with a bowling ball.[5]

Nevertheless, Bob was an interesting boy and he made a few friends who shared his favorite pastimes. In fourth grade, he and his friend Randy held Monopoly marathons on Saturdays.[6] Later on, in junior high, his friend Norm turned him on to jazz and French actress Brigitte Bardot, whose movies played at the local art house that Norm's father owned.[7]

In high school, Bob displayed some musical talent. He tried playing the clarinet in the school's marching band until he realized that he actually could not play when he was marching. So Bob joined the school chorus instead.[8]

Throughout junior high school, Bob continued to produce his publications. He always had wonderful titles, like *Tales to Drive You Batty*, *Whammy*, *Bozos on Patrol*, *Stine's Line*, *BARF*, and *FEEF*.[9] With titles like these, Bob did not have to look far for an audience. His classmates were always willing to oblige. Bob's fictitious characters, such as Harvey Poobah, who fell from the Empire State Building and survived until he struck the pavement, provided just the right kind of corn that his adolescent peers found amusing. His friends' laughter inspired him to continue writing.

Bob's magazines made the rounds in class. One of his longest creations was *From Here to Insanity*.[10] In one of the seven issues, Bob wrote a story titled "How to Read This Magazine in Class." Needless to say, the article made readers laugh. In particular, there was one part that advised any reader who got caught to tell the teacher that he or she was reading a pocket dictionary. One day, a disgruntled teacher confiscated the issue and sent Bob to see the principal.[11]

Bob's trips to the school office did not keep him from pursuing his greatest ambition, and his good grades always kept him in favorable standing. Bob was generally focused and his razor-sharp wit made him a likable guy. That is not to say that Bob did not have a few minor distractions in high school. After all, he was a healthy American boy. How could he resist the fun of fast cars and pretty girls?

CHAPTER 6

FAST CARS AND GIRLS

One of Bob Stine's best pals in high school was Jeff. Bob and Jeff had several things in common. Both were very good students with high grades, and they both loved tooling around Bexley in Jeff's little car. Having a car and a driver's license meant freedom for the two high school chums. They spent hours and hours just driving around town and frequenting the local drive-in restaurants.[1]

Jeff was interested in politics, so he ran for president of their senior class. Bob naturally became his friend's campaign manager. In his inimitable style, Bob put his comic prowess to work. He created the lampoon slogan, "Kick the Scoundrel In!" and, of course, Jeff was soundly defeated.[2]

Fortunately, Jeff shared Bob's wry sense of humor. They both had a talent for inventing personalities and acting out comedy bits. The two funnymen spent many afternoons recording their hilarious routines on their reel-to-reel tape recorders.[3]

Bob was generally content during his high school years. He and his two closest friends, Jeff and Norm, went to the movies and concerts and school sporting events. They also consumed a great deal of their favorite food: pizza. But inwardly, Bob could not shake the feeling that he was living the life of an outsider in a community where he did not belong.

This became painfully clear when Bob fell head-over-heels for his first girlfriend. The problem for Bob was that her family had a lot of money and a very big house. To make matters worse, when his girlfriend turned sixteen, her parents gave her a very expensive car. Bob was especially aware that his own little worn-out vehicle, which belonged to

> **[Stine] had a talent for inventing personalities and acting out comedy bits.**

his dad, did not look like much next to her brand-new Thunderbird.[4] He also knew that he could not afford the trendy clothes that all the other guys wore.

In *It Came From Ohio!*, Stine recalled how he felt during this time: "Imagine how nerdy I felt driving up her long driveway to pick her up on a Saturday night in my dad's beat-up little Ford."[5]

Through it all, Bob maintained his jokester persona. The teachers could often count on his facetious contributions during class, although he still could not count on their praise or appreciation.

Many years later, Stine ran into a former teacher who recognized him. "I was back in my home town, Columbus, Ohio, doing a book signing," he said, "and this woman came up to me that I didn't remember at all. She said, 'I was your English teacher. It's me, Bob. Remember, sophomore English?'" Stine did not remember her at all, but he did not want to hurt her feelings. "You were such a big influence on me," Stine said to her. "It made her day. And it was a nice thing to do."[6]

As gracious as he was in that interaction, Stine generally feels that his creative side was not given much support in high school. However, he does remember one teacher who validated his ability to write.

"Actually, later in high school the adviser to the newspaper said, 'I bet you could write a really fine column,' and [that teacher] gave me a column in the newspaper every month. That was nice. It was the first time I was ever published. It was a nice thing," Stine recalled.[7]

Stine also believes that his mother cared about what he was doing. She supported his attempts to write a serious adult novel, but he thought of himself as a high school kid without any serious ideas for the story. Bob salvaged that work by turning it into a funny animal story called *Lovable Bear*.[8]

As Bob neared the end of his senior year in high school, he put his writing talents to the test. He wrote a senior-class skit called "TV PROGRAMS THAT HAVE DISTRACTED US AND KEPT US FROM STUDYING WHILE WE WERE IN HIGH SCHOOL."[9] It was performed in front of the entire graduating class, and it was a big hit.

The fact that his peers laughed and cheered him on gave Bob just the right boost of confidence he needed for the next step in his career. Bob Stine headed to college and *Sundial* magazine.

Chapter 7

The Scariest Job of All

All through high school, Stine dreamed of writing for *Sundial*, Ohio State University's student humor magazine. Stine greatly admired some of *Sundial*'s famous graduates.

James Thurber, best known as a humor writer and cartoonist for the *New Yorker*, attended Ohio State from 1914 to 1917.[1] While there, he was *Sundial*'s editor-in-chief. Milton Caniff, originator of the successful comic strips "Steve Canyon" and "Terry and the Pirates," was art editor for the magazine in the early 1930s.

Stine was elated when he found out he was accepted at OSU. He looked forward to spending more time doing what he wanted. He would study English and write.

Stine expected college life to be different from high school. However, some things about everyday living would be the same.

"I lived at home during college," Stine explained. "My brother and I actually shared the top floor of this little house. Can you imagine? I was at home. He was like my roommate in college."[2]

But Stine did not plan on spending many of his college days in his childhood residence. He immediately set his sights on becoming a member of *Sundial*'s staff. The magazine's office soon became his headquarters and center of operations.

Stine was thrilled to be following in the footsteps of the celebrated alumni he admired, though it did not take long before he had higher goals. By the end of his freshman year, Stine wanted to be editor, not just a writer for the magazine. He knew his mischievous reputation preceded him, so he treaded cautiously. Stine did everything he could to convince

> **"I lived at home during college. My brother . . . was like my roommate in college."**
> **—R. L. Stine**

the OSU publications board that he could do the job, and it worked.[3]

As editor, Bob's objective was to publish a monthly humor magazine that was packed with laughs, fake interviews, phony ads, and cartoons that spoofed and mocked college life. This was right up Stine's alley. Nothing was sacred. Campus rules, curfews, and faculty were often the brunt of *Sundial*'s jokes.[4]

The twenty-five-cent magazine was especially popular with the young men on campus. Each month it featured a photo of a coed as "Girl of the Month." One month Stine actually printed a photo of a real rising young movie star. *Sundial*'s sales sky-rocketed. Eight thousand copies of the magazine were sold in just one day.[5]

During his three years as editor, Stine went by the name Jovial Bob, who was also a recurring *Sundial* character.[6] During his senior year, Jovial Bob ran for the Student Senate. He used campaigners dressed in clown suits. They told the voters that since all of the candidates were clowns, they should vote for Jovial Bob, the only clown willing to admit he was one.

Stine was up to his old tricks. In fact, Jovial Bob was not eligible to run for the presidency because his alter ego, Stine, was graduating before the new term. Nonetheless, Jovial Bob received more than a thousand votes by promising the student body "nothing."[7]

It seems that controversy followed Stine wherever he went. College life was no exception. Ohio State's student newspaper, the *Lantern*, criticized Jovial Bob's satirical writing and tongue-in-cheek campus antics. The *Lantern* often gave *Sundial*, as Stine put it, "downright nasty" reviews.[8]

After graduation, Stine was ready to go to New York to pursue his writing career. He still dreamed about having his own humor magazine and thought New York would be the place to achieve his goal.

"When I was in junior high school, my friends and I, all of us, that's all we talked about, about how we were going to leave Ohio and go to New York. Every day we would talk about New York and how we would get there. But I, of course, really believed that if you wanted to be a writer, you had to live in Greenwich Village. I was the only one who made it. No one else came. They all went different places. No one else came to New York."[9]

Only one thing stood in Stine's way. Relocating to New York required money. Stine did not have any. So he took a job as a substitute teacher—a job, as Stine described it, scarier than robbing banks. "I can't imagine anything more horrifying than facing a new class of students each and every morning," he wrote in *It Came From Ohio!*[10]

Stine needed the work, so he took the job. Within a few months, he was offered a position teaching history. It was not exactly a perfect match for an English major, but having his own class would be better than substituting and a perfect opportunity

> **During his three years as editor [of the *Sundial*], Stine went by the name Jovial Bob, who was also a recurring *Sundial* character.**

to save up some money while observing young adults.[11]

Not surprisingly, Stine taught history to the beat of his own drum. He was not expecting to win any accolades for his unorthodox practices. For example, Stine allowed his students free reading time on Fridays. Hoping to stimulate their interest in printed material, he let them choose whatever they wanted to read. Sometimes this included comics.[12]

Fortunately, Stine's supervisor only gave him disapproving looks, and Stine survived his first and only year of teaching. All the while his zeal for comic books never waned.

Stine's scariest job of all was short-lived, but he came away with a wealth of valuable observations about teens and how they walk, and talk, and behave. He would put that knowledge to good use in due time.

While teaching, Stine did two important things. He continued to write, and he saved his money.

Stine revived his horn-rimmed-glasses-wearing superhero, Captain Anything, hoping to sell the two-minute comedy scripts to radio shows all over the country.[13]

The scripts did not sell well. Still, in the autumn of 1966, Stine packed up and took off for the Big Apple.

Chapter 8

Biting the Big Apple

"I had four hundred dollars to my name. I came to New York and moved to an apartment in Greenwich Village. I had to do that. I did not think any different. I actually did it. I'm amazed that I did it. I had no money. I didn't know a single person in the city, and I just did it. I got a horrible apartment down on Waverly Place and started reading *The Times*, looking for jobs. I was going around getting magazine jobs. I was pretty brave, I think. It wasn't like coming from Russia, but I did everything on my own."[1]

Stine was enamored with the city. He loved the late-night shopping and the coffeehouses and the bookstores, but he did not love living on bologna sandwiches. He needed money to survive. Stine needed employment.

In his tiny one-room apartment, Stine combed through the classifieds for opportunities to write.

After an incompatible trial with *Institutional Investor*, a magazine dealing with the stock market, Stine came across a job with his name written all over it. He spoke with an editor who managed a group of fan magazines. The editor needed someone to write imaginary interviews. Stine knew he could do this with his eyes shut, and he was pleased that the position would pay one hundred dollars a week. He landed the job and went right to work. Within one month, Stine wrote fictitious interviews about dozens of 1960s music celebrities, such as Glen Campbell, the Rolling Stones, the Beatles, and Diana Ross and the Supremes.[2]

Stine caught another lucky break when his editor's boss started up a new magazine called *Adventures in Horror*. When Stine was not making up interviews, he was writing otherworldly tales under the name Robert Lawrence.[3] However, Stine did not envision himself as a horror writer. The new role was work. The good thing was that he was getting paid to write.

> **"I had four hundred dollars to my name. I came to New York . . . I'm amazed that I did it."**
> **—R. L. Stine**

Stine ate much better with the money he earned. Then the magazine venture dissolved, and Stine was back to the drawing board and bologna sandwiches.

His next job was for *Soft Drink Industry* magazine.[4] It provided "bread and butter," but writing articles about soda, soda cans, soda syrup, and the people who work in the soda business did not quench Stine's professional thirst. Stine's lack of interest in *Soft Drink Industry* kept him on the look-out for other writing gigs.

It was not all bad. At least Stine was working in the Big Apple and the Big Apple was working for Stine. He had a place to live, he had a job (even though it was not exactly what he wanted), and he still had his driving ambition. What more could he want?

How about *Bananas*?

CHAPTER 9

BANANAS AND
A HOT DATE

Stine met Jane Waldhorn at a friend's party on a rainy night in Brooklyn, New York. Waldhorn's long red hair and beautiful blue-gray eyes caught Stine's attention. They were married a few months later on June 22, 1969.[1]

Bob and Jane both started working as staff writers for Scholastic, Inc., one of the leading publishing houses in New York. Bob Stine contributed news and history articles to *Junior Scholastic*, a popular current events magazine.[2] Jane Stine wrote real interviews with famous people for *Scope*, a magazine for middle-grade students.[3]

Stine liked the fast pace of working on a weekly publication. He enjoyed the challenge of writing interesting articles and presenting them in creative ways that appealed to reluctant junior high school readers. He drew on his experiences as a history

Robert and Jane Stine on their wedding day, June 22, 1969.

teacher and his activities as a punster at *Sundial*. Stine knew that humor was a great way to reach his audience, particularly boys who tended to have very distinct reading interests.

What Stine knew about readers served him well when he moved up to become editor of *Search*, an easy-reading social studies magazine for less-than-enthusiastic, middle-grade readers.[4]

Jane Stine was also advancing at Scholastic. She accepted an editorial position with one of the company's other teen publications, *Dynamite*.[5]

There was something about Bob Stine and Scholastic that just clicked. When the company offered him the chance to be the editor of *Bananas*, he could not refuse. Stine remembered it this way:

"I did this humor magazine called *Bananas* for ten years. This was my life's ambition. That was my dream. I would have paid them. I couldn't believe I had my own national humor magazine."[6]

Bananas was a publishing triumph for Stine and for Scholastic. It was hugely popular, and it allowed him to do exactly what he wanted to do: make people laugh. Of course, the magazine was chock-full of madcap articles, jokes, and interviews, all reflecting Jovial Bob's unconventional comic slant.

Everything at Scholastic was going well for Stine when he got a phone call from Ellen Rudin, a children's book editor at E. P. Dutton. She wanted to give Stine, a.k.a. Jovial Bob, a contract to write a funny book for children. Stine dove right in. Dutton published *How To Be Funny* in 1978. It was Stine's first published book for children.[7]

Stine showed up for his first book signing wearing bunny ears. Passersby looked at him curiously, not quite sure what to make of a grown man in a rabbit costume. Jovial Bob signed and sold only one book that day, a sharp contrast to the book sales in his future.[8]

Stine continued to edit *Bananas*. Then, suddenly, Scholastic's financial situation changed and the publisher decided to downsize. Once again, Stine rallied to the challenge. He moved over from *Bananas* and took responsibility for starting a new magazine called *Maniac*.[9] Within a year, Stine was out of a job completely. He remembered it like this:

"I really thought I had filled my life's ambition, and I would just coast. I was like 39 years old, and I thought, I've done it. Great! I was making a nice living, nothing great, but we'd been breaking even. Jane and I had no idea what was in store."[10]

During the time that Stine was editing *Bananas*, he was also writing joke books with catchy titles like *The Beast Handbook* and *The Cool Kids' Guide to Summer Camp*. Not long after *Bananas* collapsed, Stine was freelancing full-time. He wrote more joke books, composed lots of *Choose Your Own Adventure* stories, and became a staff writer for a cable TV show on Nickelodeon called *Eureka's Castle*.[11]

"I wrote bubble gum cards," Stine said. "I wrote Mighty Mouse Coloring Books. I wrote G. I. Joe novels, even though I'd never seen a gun."[12]

Stine even did some writing with his wife, Jane. "When Jane and I first started out, we wrote together," said Stine. "We collaborated on a bunch of funny books for kids." But the joint effort was unsuccessful.

"It didn't work at all," Stine added. "I have to write the first word, then the second. I have to write in total order. Jane would write the ending. Then she would go back and write part of the middle. Then she'd go back and rewrite it. Then she'd go back to the beginning. It drove me nuts. I couldn't do it. Jane loves to revise and rewrite."[13]

Although Stine and his wife collaborated on some books, nothing compared to the joint creation they produced on June 7, 1980, when Matthew Daniel Stine was born.[14]

Bob Stine loved being a parent and the nature of his work made it possible for him to become a full-time, stay-at-home, book-writing dad. Matthew and his dad were very close, but Stine remembers that

> "I really thought I had filled my life's ambition [as editor of *Bananas*]. . . . I thought, I've done it."
> —R. L. Stine

the young Matt refused to read any of his father's books.

However, Matt did share his father's appreciation for comic books. Stine remembers how important they were during Matthew's childhood.

"My son read only *Garfield* comics all his life. He never read one of my books, never. He had the whole *Garfield* collection. We [Stine and his wife] never said a word. We let him read every night."[15]

While Bob Stine was home writing, Jane Stine and her colleague Joan Waricha were busy with their new publishing company, Parachute Press. This soon became a vehicle for circulating Stine's freelance

R. L. Stine holds his son, Matthew.

projects, but, more important, Parachute Press would own and edit Stine's work.[16]

"You know," said Stine, "my wife is one of my editors. And she is very tough. I always say she is like a hockey goalie. Nothing gets past her. Nothing! That's very good."[17]

For the first time, Stine was using a computer to write. He enjoyed his job as head writer for *Eureka's Castle*. He also liked that it got him out of the house. The entertaining TV show featuring puppets won several Nickelodeon Kid's Choice Awards for best children's program. This was a feather in Stine's cap. Once again, he proved that he had the talent to amuse young audiences.

Then Stine got another phone call. This time it was for a very scary date.

CHAPTER 10

GOOSEBUMPS AND GHOSTS

"That's how I got started. It wasn't even my idea. Who knew? It came as a total shock to us," said Stine, referring to the phone call that changed the course of his life.[1]

What happened? "That's easy," Stine responds. "This editor asked me to write a horror novel. That was it. At that point, I was home. I was a freelance writer, and I would never say no to anything. People would call you and want you to do something and you would always say yes to whatever it was."[2]

Stine agreed to meet with former Scholastic editor-in-chief Jean Feiwel. She asked him to go home and write a horror novel for teenagers called *Blind Date*. He did not know what she was talking about, but he agreed to do it.[3]

Stine went to the bookstore to find out what he was supposed to do. He got some books by Joan

Lowery Nixon, Christopher Pike, and Lois Duncan. Then he read them all. He noted what it was that he liked about them and what he did not like. Stine decided that he would go for a slightly younger audience.

"I wanted my books to be a little cleaner, a little safer. They wouldn't go quite as far, and they would have some humor in them," explained Stine.[4]

With his goal defined, Stine went home and spent three months writing *Blind Date*. Stine handed in a manuscript about a boy who gets a mysterious phone call from a girl. She tells him that she is his blind date. The girl turns out to be dead, and the story is very creepy.

> "I wanted my books to be a little cleaner, a little safer."
> —R. L. Stine

Blind Date came out in 1986. In no time, it was the number-one young-adult best-seller in *Publisher's Weekly*.[5] This achievement amazed Stine. "I said, wait a minute. I never had a number-one best-seller. What's going on here?"[6]

The other amazing thing about *Blind Date* is that it sold well to both girls and boys. Stine realized he had struck a chord in a brand-new market.

"I always loved horror," he said. "When my brother and I were kids back in the fifties, we used to go to all the scary movies. I loved them, but I never thought about writing them. I was always a funny guy. And now I found something that the kids really liked."[7]

Feiwel wanted Stine to write one teen horror

book a year. His next two books were *Twisted*, a story about a group of sorority members who commit murders, and *The Baby-Sitter*, about a baby-sitter who receives phone calls that threaten her safety. Both books also became young-adult best-sellers.

Stine saw the possibility of making a living writing and selling horror books for teens, and he thought he could do a whole series. He came up with the idea for *Fear Street*.[8]

Jane Stine and Joan Waricha of Parachute Press took the proposal for the *Fear Street* series to Pocket Books. Stine signed on to do three books and then three more.[9] *The New Girl* got the series started. It was followed by *The Surprise Party* and *The Overnight*.

Stine's popularity with ten-to-fourteen-year-olds took off. The first three books produced an avalanche of best-sellers. He immersed himself in *Fear Street* and wrote one book a month. The kids loved the books, and Stine was mystified.

Even though the books were filled with lots of terror and some characters died, Stine believed that his readers knew it was not real. "I was very careful to make sure that it was like a fantasy," he said. "They didn't have a lot of the real world in them. No divorce, no drugs, no child abuse, no anything that would hurt the fantasy. I didn't want them really believing it, and I didn't really want to scare kids."[10]

The *Fear Street* series sold wonderfully, and Stine had plenty to keep him busy. Doing another series at the time was the furthest thing from his mind. When his wife and her partner at Parachute Press, Joan Waricha, approached him about doing something for the middle-grade audience, he was not interested.

R. L. Stine waits to sign copies of his books during a book-signing appearance.

"They wanted me to do a younger series of scary books, and I said I didn't want to jeopardize *Fear Street*. *Fear Street* was doing so well I didn't want to go to a younger audience and make *Fear Street* not cool. So I put it off."[11]

Parachute Press saw an opportunity that Stine himself did not see at the time. The two editors kept after him, and finally Stine gave in on the condition that he would try it if he could think of a good name for the series.

"One day," said Stine," I was reading *TV Guide*, going through the listings. There was an ad on the bottom of the page that said it was Goosebumps week on channel 11 and that they were showing all these scary movies. There it was. There was the title. It was perfect."[12]

Stine and Parachute Press immediately shared the idea of a *Goosebumps* series with Scholastic. Right away, Scholastic bought six titles.

Goosebumps was conceived as a series of creepy fantasies with a lot of funny stuff in them so they would never get too scary. This meant that if the story got too intense, Stine would throw in something funny.

"The first book (*Welcome to the Dead House*) is a little too scary, I think," said Stine. "I thought it was just too creepy. And then with the second one, *Stay Out of the Basement*, about a father who turns into a plant, I had it right."[13]

Up to that point, there had never been anything like *Goosebumps* in publishing. Stine had no idea what would happen next.

"I'd go visit schools and I'd say to the kids, 'Why do you like these books?' And they'd say, 'We like to be scared.' That was always the answer. 'We like to be scared.' And I figured out that they like to be scared when they know that they're safe at the same time. So we started calling these books safe scared," Stine explained.[14]

Stine wrote a typical *Goosebumps* book in about ten days. "I do a lot of planning before I start to write. For every book I do, I do a complete chapter-by-chapter outline," he said. "Kids hate to hear that.

> "The first book . . . is a little too scary. . . . [T]he second one . . . I had it right."
> —R. L. Stine

Nobody likes to outline. But I can't work without it now. I do chapter one and everything that's going to happen in the chapter. I do twenty to twenty-five-page outlines. When I sit down to write, I know everything that's going to happen in the book so I can just sit back, relax, and enjoy the writing. And that's why I can write so fast."[15]

"Fast" is one word to describe what Stine has accomplished. In about two years, he wrote eighty-seven *Goosebumps* books. At one point, four million *Goosebumps* were sold each month. About two hundred and forty million *Goosebumps* and about eighty million *Fear Street* books have been sold to date.[16]

Stine's success with *Goosebumps* and *Fear Street* was riddled with controversy. The *Goosebumps* series was number sixteen on The 100 Most Frequently Challenged Books of 1990–2000.[17]

R. L. Stine makes friends on the set of the television show inspired by his book series of the same name, *Goosebumps*.

"Since 1990, the American Library Association's (ALA) Office for Intellectual Freedom (OIF) has recorded more than 7,800 book challenges, including 458 in 2003. A challenge is a formal, written complaint requesting a book be removed from library shelves or school curriculum. About three out of four of all challenges are to material in schools or school libraries, and one in four are to material in public libraries. . . . The most challenged and/or restricted reading materials have been books for children."[18]

Outspoken critics claimed that children who read horror would be adversely affected. They also believed that Stine's work was not academically challenging enough and that children should be reading "good quality, cultured literature" instead. The attackers questioned the "redeeming value" of Stine's "shock fiction," and proposed that reading this kind of series fiction would have a harmful effect on children's reading in general.

Many supporters came to Stine's defense. In his book, *What's So Scary About R. L. Stine?*, author and librarian Patrick Jones pointed out: "An award-winning research project by Dr. Catherine Sheldrick Ross found that series reading, far from being harmful, might be for some readers an essential stage in their development as powerful readers."[19]

Dr. Ross noted: "Discourse on popular fiction has changed very little over the past one hundred years, as becomes evident if we compare what was said about 'trashy' fiction and dime novels in the 1800s with what is being said now about the horror series for young readers."[20]

Generations of children had been reading series fiction and loving it. *Tom Swift*, *Cherry Ames*, *Nancy Drew*, *The Hardy Boys*, and *The Bobbsey Twins* had been successful series that were popular, reasonably priced entertainment. More importantly, kids read them.

During the heat of the debate in 1996, Secretary of Education Richard Riley said, "All of our research tells us that this is so important. Read a book, read the sports page, read the comics or read R. L. Stine's *Goosebumps* and get excited together—it doesn't matter. Just read."[21]

Recent supporters continue to point out the value of series fiction. Jim Trelease, author of *The Read-Aloud Handbook* (Penguin Putnam, 2001), favors series fiction books because, simply, kids read them. It gives them an "instant start."[22]

"His books serve a purpose: they entertain," Jones wrote in his book about Stine. "But more than that," he said, "they give kids a positive reading experience to which they can respond since the horror is fun, yet also familiar. While it might be easy to suggest that anyone could have written these books, the fact that Stine has outsold and outlasted almost everyone else working in this genre demonstrates that his genius is special and worthy of serious study."[23]

So what does Stine think of all the fuss? "This talk of complaints about what it was, that it wasn't literature, that they should be reading uplifting stuff never really went very far," he said. "Funny, we live in modern times. It's impossible to get kids to read. If a parent finds something that kids actually like to read, it's a wonderful thing for them. . . . Many of the same people who complained about *Goosebumps*, complained about Harry Potter."[24]

Stine contends that his books are healthy for kids because they allow them to cope with their own

Stine signs the title page of one of his *Goosebumps* books for a fan at a book-signing event.

anger and repressed feelings. Stine also believes that his readers are intelligent and that they can tell the difference between a fictional scare and real life.

Stine's series books maintained their popularity, and they sold well. His titles continued to make news as good reads. In 2004, the American Library Association chose Stine's *Dangerous Girls* as one of their Quick Picks for Reluctant Young Adult Readers.

In 2004, Stine released a sequel to *Dangerous Girls* called *The Taste of Night*, from HarperCollins, and a new adult thriller called *Eye Candy*, from Ballantine Books. Then Stine followed these with still another new series called *Mostly Ghostly* for readers ages seven to eleven.

In *Mostly Ghostly*, the main character, Max, finds himself dealing with two ghosts who suddenly show up in his house. The ghosts do not know how they became ghosts, and Max is the only one who can see them. Stine drew his idea for this series from another favorite childhood movie, a supernatural comedy from 1937 called *Topper*.

Mostly Ghostly was something different for Stine. It marked the first time that he ever did a continuing story. "Every book I've ever done," he said, "I've started all over again with a whole new cast of characters. In *Goosebumps*, every month there was a new story and a whole new cast of characters. In *Mostly Ghostly*, there are the same characters, Max, the two ghosts, Nicky and Tara, and an evil spirit named Phears."[25]

What's next for Stine? Only time will tell. Does he ever get tired of writing? "Only when I'm revising," he confessed. "I don't have the same energy for revising as I do for writing. But I don't think any writer does. I do a lot of revising. Otherwise I still look forward to getting up in the morning and starting a new book. I still enjoy it a lot."[26]

When he is not writing, Stine reads. He loves quaint English mysteries by Agatha Christie, Ruth Rendell, and M.C. Beaton. Stine shared these

> **"I don't have the same energy for revising as I do for writing. But I don't think any writer does."**
> **—R. L. Stine**

thoughts about his favorite author, the English humorist P. G. Wodehouse: "I love his writing. I can't believe the plotting, the amazing plotting, and the amazing language. You just wanted to be in that world. He is really a hero of mine. He lived to be ninety-three, and he wrote ninety-three books."[27] Stine is proud of his collection of first editions of Wodehouse's novels.

Stine also holds American author Ray Bradbury in high esteem. Stine remembers Bradbury's effect on him as a boy. "My other hero is Ray Bradbury. When I was about ten years old, he turned me into a reader. I read only comic books up until that time. Then, when I was nine or ten, I discovered Ray Bradbury's short stories and I just couldn't believe it. They were so imaginative and had so many surprises and great twist endings. I just love them."[28] When Stine was nineteen, he read Bradbury's *Something Wicked This Way Comes*. That story had a powerful impact on Stine's own scary storytelling.

Stine is very proud of *Beware*, a collection of

short scary stories by his favorite authors. For Stine it was a thrill to put all his favorite people into an anthology. The volume includes "The Black Ferris," by Ray Bradbury. "I put his story up front and dedicated the book to Ray Bradbury. He sent me the nicest letter . . . the most wonderful letter, and ended it 'yours in admiration.' What a thing to get from someone who's your hero."[29]

In addition, Stine said, "[Another] very big influence on me was *Pinocchio*. When I was very little, my mother would read to me before naptime. The original *Pinocchio* was unbelievably violent. At one point, Pinocchio takes a wooden mallet and he smashes Jiminy Cricket against a wall and crushes him. Then Pinocchio falls asleep with his feet on the stove and he burns his feet off. I still remember this, all this time later. So, I think that was very influential on me. It stayed in my mind . . . the violence and the horror of *Pinocchio*."[30]

> "[Bradbury] turned me into a reader. I read only comic books up until that time."
>
> —R. L. Stine

Stine says that several of his favorite *Goosebumps* books reflect the hold that this fairy tale had on him. "I like all the ones with Slappy, the evil dummy . . . *Night of the Living Dummy* and *Night of the Living Dummy 2* . . . just because I was always fascinated with puppets and dummies and things like that."[31]

Stine also loved the science fiction shows on television in the 1960s. In 1999, Parachute Press and HarperCollins Children's Books published a collection of ten of Stine's short stories. Many of the stories in *The Nightmare Hour* have "surprise" endings in the tradition of *The Twilight Zone*, one of Stine's favorite TV programs from his youth. Stine followed *The Nightmare Hour* with another series, called *The Nightmare Room*, a quieter, darker series where there are no monsters. The stories are psychological. The reader enters a familiar place that is not quite what was expected.

"Kids barely noticed *The Nightmare Room*," said Stine. "They were still reading *Goosebumps* and would walk right by it. *The Nightmare Room* was not a big success at all, even with *The Nightmare Room* TV series."[32]

Chapter 11

Just a Regular Guy

Stine is especially proud of the literacy work he does for children. He sponsors the R. L. Stine Writing Workshop at all three elementary schools in his hometown of Bexley, Ohio. Every year, a published author spends two weeks at each school and works instructively with the kids who want to be writers. The program serves hundreds of students.[1]

Along with *The Nightmare Room* series, Stine created *The Nightmare Room* website, where visitors can find *The Nightmare Room* screensaver, read an exclusive on-line story, or create their own personal interactive nightmare. The site also offers a free writing program that teachers can download and use in their classrooms.[2]

"It's free," said Stine referring to the writing program. "Any teacher can print it out for the whole class. I've done some writing workshops from that. I've gone into five or six classrooms and done it and had a lot of fun with it. It's really good work."[3]

Stine also attends many literary benefits to promote literacy, and he often makes appearances all around the world. In February, 2001, Stine helped Governor Jeb Bush kick off a literacy campaign in the state of Florida. Stine was also the visiting author at Public School 3, in New York City, during the school's 2002 writing festival.

Then, in October, 2003, Laura Bush, wife of President George W. Bush, invited Stine and two other American authors to go with her to Moscow for the Russian Book Festival.[4] Stine was asked to go because of his general fame and because he is very popular with the children in Russia. With the help of an interpreter, Stine read to an audience of Russian children and Russian librarians.[5] He also asked for ideas from the audience and used them to invent a chilling tale about a boy and a haunted car.

"I got to fly on her [Laura Bush's] plane," Stine reminisced. "It was an amazing time. We spent a week with her in Moscow, and I met the Putins and Mrs. Blair [wife of the prime minister of England]. I gave a little talk to the Russian kids. And I also had dinner in the Kremlin and front row seats at the Bolshoi. It was incredible. I had to say, 'Whose life is this?'"[6]

These days Stine enjoys living in the spacious Manhattan apartment that he and his family moved into in 1996. Now there is plenty of room for his office and his pool table and his pinball machine, and, of course, Nadine, the Stines' dog. There is also room for his books and his collection of first editions.

Today, R. L. Stine enjoys living in New York with family.

Stine speaks lovingly about his family and appreciatively about his good fortune. He hopes to continue writing, traveling, and living in New York. "I can't imagine living anywhere else," he said, while enjoying lunch at one of his favorite neighborhood bistros.[7]

As attached as Stine is to the Big Apple, he has never used the city as a setting for any of his books for children.

"I've never written a children's book that takes place in Manhattan," he said. "That started because I wanted my books to take place in backyards and houses, normal locales. I thought that would be more frightening for kids. As time went by, I became superstitious about it and wouldn't write any New York stories. However, when it came to doing my adult thrillers in the past two years, I decided to turn around completely. They both take place in New York and the Hamptons."

So how does he stay so humble? "My family, mainly," he admits. "When I go home, I'm 'shut-up you jerk.' That's my name. I don't know. It happened so late. I'd been writing for kids for twenty-five years. And then *Goosebumps* came along. So I have twenty-five years of nobody noticing me. I always remember those times."

Stine thinks of himself as just a regular guy. "I did everything on my own," he says. "I don't know what else to be really. I never act like a celebrity. I never forget how lucky I am."[8]

IN HIS OWN WORDS

The following interview was conducted with R. L. Stine by the author on May 20, 2004.

How did you decide to use the name R. L. Stine?

When I was writing the funny books, I was Jovial Bob Stine. I was Jovial Bob in college when I did the college humor magazine, *Bananas*. All the funny books are Jovial Bob Stine. And when I wrote *Eureka's Castle*, the TV series, I was Jovial Bob. Then when I wrote *Blind Date*, Jovial Bob was not appropriate. So I just used my initials.

So it was your idea to use just your initials?

Yes.

Why not use your entire name, Robert Lawrence Stine?

At that time, S. E. Hinton was selling a lot of books for teenagers. They were very popular. And we thought we were writing this series for girls. So I thought by using my initials they wouldn't know if it was a man or a woman. That's why I started using my initials. It's sort of my more dignified name. It was more appropriate than Jovial Bob.

Is there anyone who still calls you "Bobby"?

I actually have one cousin, Marsha, who I hadn't seen in forty years. I recently reunited with her. She still calls me Bobby. She's the last person in the world. I can't get her to stop.

When did you become Bob?

I guess junior high or high school.

How did you make the transition from comedy to horror?

That's a good question. I think they're very closely related. Maybe you have this same experience. When I go to a horror show or when I go to a scary movie, it always makes me laugh. I never get scared. I always think it's funny. When you go to a theme park and you walk up close to a roller coaster and you hear the people on the roller coaster, you hear them screaming and laughing at the same time. I think there is a very close connection between the two.

Do you ever have any nightmares like the ones you write?

I never have nightmares. When I started writing scary books, I never had another nightmare. I guess it's because I could get it out during the day. I have the most boring dreams you can imagine. One night I dreamed I was making a bologna sandwich. And that was like really exciting. I got out the bread, I went to the refrigerator. . . . No, I never have nightmares.

When you were in junior high school, you dreamed not only about becoming a writer, but about living in New York. Now that you've lived in New York for more than thirty-five years, is there any of the Ohio boy left in you?

Well, there are still cousins and everything back there. My wife is from Long Island, New York. I can't imagine living anywhere else but New York.

I just couldn't imagine it. I just love it. I've been here for over thirty-five years. I never get tired of it. You can take a walk and see so many things . . . people, the arts, theater.

For a long time you, your wife, and your son lived in a very small apartment. What was that like?

We lived in a little apartment for twenty-six years. We had a teenager and one bathroom. That was a horror story.

Where is your son now?

Matty had to get out of the city for a little while. He went to school in Wisconsin for audio engineering and learned everything about sound. But he's a real New Yorker now. He's half living at home and half living in the Village in an apartment. He set up a whole recording studio and people come in and he records demos for them. He is also a sound designer for a theater in Westchester. He does all the sound effects for the plays and he writes original music.

Your mother always supported your interest in writing when you were young. What does she think of your work now?

I sent my mom *The Sitter*, and she said, "Bob, did you use words you shouldn't use?"

Do you ever get tired of touring?

No. I love that part. It's a thrill to get out of the house. And I love seeing the kids. In fact, I can't do too much of it and do the number of books that I do. A lot of authors do one book a year. And then they can tour a couple of months. One book a year and that's it . . . tour for a couple of months and then spend the next six months doing another one. But I can't do that. I'm doing a big tour in the fall. I really enjoy that part a lot.

What is it that you enjoy about touring?

I used to do book signings at Disney World every Halloween. And I'd say, "You could be out having fun. Why are you waiting in line for me? You spend an hour waiting in line for me when you could be out riding things." It's incredible. The last time I was at the *L.A. Times* Book Festival, which is my favorite book festival—it's on the UCLA campus, I got to be with 400 authors. I never know what to expect now because I'm not the hottest author in the world. There are so many selling better than me now. There was a wonderful crowd. Hundreds of kids lined up. It's such a thrill every time. Every time. To think that people would stand in line.

Has anything particularly special happened to you during a book signing?

I was in Dallas, and I was pretty tired. I had been touring for quite a while. I signed a book for this little blond boy, this angelic little blond boy. I signed the book for him, shook hands, and talked with him a little bit. And as he went off this long line, he turned to his mother with an incredible look on his face. And he said, "I'm the luckiest man on earth." And I just burst into tears. I still can't tell it without tearing up. It was this unbelievable moment. It was just incredible. And I had to run back behind the shelves to get it together. It was very bad for my image, standing there crying. So that's why I love touring. I love the children.

You recently had a very unique opportunity to go to Russia with First Lady Laura Bush. Did the Russian children know you? Did they know your work?

Yeah. Actually, *The Nightmare Room* books are very popular in Russia right now.

What was it like meeting Laura Bush?

Mrs. Bush was very down to earth. It was a real thrill. And it turned out that the Bush twins, the two girls, grew up on *Goosebumps*. So Laura Bush said that they had *Goosebumps* all over the house. The girls loved them.

How do parents respond to you?

When I do book tours, when I go out, parents are so grateful. Parents are wonderful everywhere I go. They say, "Thank you, my boy learned to read on this. Thank you. My kid never read a book in his life. Last night I caught him with a flashlight reading your book." Everywhere I go. It's a wonder. I never get tired of hearing it.

Were you ever really concerned about the controversy that surrounded Goosebumps?

This talk of complaints about what it was, that it wasn't literature, they should be reading uplifting stuff, it never really went very far. My son read only *Garfield* comics all his life. He never read one of my books, never. He read only *Garfield*. He had the collection. We never said a word. We let him read every night. He went off to college. He was an English major. He read *Ulysses*. He went from *Garfield* to *Ulysses*. Go figure.

You said that Ray Bradbury was influential in making you a reader as a young boy. Did you ever meet him?

I just loved him a lot. Every once in a while you get to meet your hero. I was at the *L.A. Times* Book Festival and there was Ray Bradbury, sitting on campus eating a hot dog. And I thought I had to go over there. I had to say something. I wanted to meet him. So I walked over, but I was nervous. I went over and said, "Mr. Bradbury, you're my hero." And we shook hands and he said, "Well, you're a hero to a lot of other people."

What do kids always ask you?

Kids always ask about what I do about writer's block. It's the most-asked question wherever I go. It's in every single letter. That's all I hear. And for a long time, I didn't take it seriously. I thought, why are they asking this question? And then I realized that kids have to write more than any living human. Most people get out of school and they never have to write again. But kids have to write every day, every week. And they really think that if you could tell them where you get your ideas from, then they'll be able to get ideas, too. And that's why we did the Writing Program. I did a writing program for kids. It's free. You can download it. And it has all my secrets. It has everything. It's a sixteen-page writing program. You can get it from www.nightmareroom.com. Click on the writing program. It's totally free. It has all kinds of stuff: how to get started; how to outline; how to get ideas; how never to have writer's block.

Where do you get new ideas?

I have to have the title first. I get most of my ideas from the title. One day I was walking the dog in the park and a title just flashed in my mind . . . *Dear Diary, I'm Dead*. So then I started to figure out what that would be about. That became a *Nightmare Room* book.

How do you get a new piece of writing started?

A lot of people think you just sit down and start writing. I tell people I can't write unless I know the end of the book. I can't write unless I know the end. At some meeting a girl told me she always gets bogged down in the middle. She asked me, "What do you do?" I said I write the end first. There's no way I could get bogged down. She was shocked. If you do all this planning in advance you can't have writer's block.

What is your writing routine like?

I write five or six days a week. I treat it like a full-time job. I'm good from about 10 A.M. to 3 P.M. Then there are no words left. I could never write at night. I get tired of the revising part. I have a lot of editors, and I find it very helpful. Otherwise I still look forward to getting up in the morning and starting a new book. I still enjoy it a lot.

What advice would you like to give to kids who want to write?

I have very boring advice for kids who want to write. One is read, read, read. Don't read one author. Read all kinds of authors. Because even without realizing, you soak up their styles, the way they write, and the language that they use. The other thing is to write something every day. Keep a journal or a diary.

Do you keep a journal or a diary?

I have a lot of e-mail pals. There are some people that I've never met that I e-mail. But I don't keep a journal or a diary. After I finish my work for the day, and I've done my ten or fifteen pages, that's it.

What else do you do during the day?

I have to walk the dog three times a day.

Do you still have the old typewriter from your childhood?

My brother has a bunch of old typewriters. Maybe he has it. I haven't seen it in years.

Do you still type with one finger?

Yes, I never learned to type correctly. I still type with only one finger (not even two!). My poor finger is totally bent and crooked and ruined from typing so many books. I figure if the finger ever gives out, there goes the career.

You certainly have made writing your life. What do you make of that?

I heard one writer say it was an addiction. I never thought of it in terms like that. But I guess that's true. I really couldn't go more than two or three weeks and not write something. It really is an addiction.

What is it that you haven't done that you'd still like to do?

I would like to have a couple of movies. I haven't had a feature film. That's one ambition. The *Goosebumps* feature never got made. I have been so lucky. How many children's authors have two TV shows? The first one, the *Goosebumps* show, was the number-one kids' show for three seasons. *The Nightmare Room* was really nice, too, but it only ran for thirteen episodes. I've done everything way beyond my dreams. I have a new adult thriller coming out; but I like writing for kids, and I don't have any ambition to write a great novel. I love what I'm doing. I've gone way beyond what I ever dreamed I'd ever do.

What do you want people to think about Bob Stine?

That's a hard question. I'm easygoing, but I'm driven at the same time. You have to be a little crazy to write three hundred books. You have to be pretty driven. I think I'm fairly easygoing and not very demanding. That about sums it up.

TIMELINE

1943—Robert Lawrence Stine is born to Lewis and Anne Stine in Columbus, Ohio, on October 8.

1952—Writes "The All New Bob Stine Giggle Book" on his first typewriter. Writes "HAH! For Maniacs Only!!"

1956—Turns thirteen and has his bar mitzvah. He receives a new typewriter as a bar mitzvah gift from his parents.

1957—Creates *From Here to Insanity*.

1958—Takes driving lessons.

1961—Enrolls at Ohio State University.

1962–1965—Is named editor of *Sundial*, the humor magazine at Ohio State. Writes satire under the name "Jovial Bob."

1965—Graduates from Ohio State University with a B.A. in English. Works as a substitute teacher.

1966—Teaches history in a junior high school in Columbus. Moves to New York City, rents an apartment in Greenwich Village, and starts writing for a living. Publishes his first horror story, "Bony Fingers from the Grave," in *Adventure in Horror*.

1966–1967—Does graduate work at New York University.

1968—Hired by Scholastic, Inc., a children's publisher, as a staff writer on *Junior Scholastic*. Later becomes an associate editor.

1969—Bob meets magazine writer Jane Waldhorn and marries her on June 22.

1972–1975—Becomes editor at *Search* magazine.

1975–1983—Creates and edits his own humor magazine, *Bananas*, for Scholastic.

1978—First children's book, *How to Be Funny*, by Jovial Bob Stine, is published by Dutton.

1980—Matthew Daniel Stine is born on June 7.

1982—First multiple-storyline book, *The Time Raider*, is published by Scholastic.

1982–1989—Publishes several more multiple-storyline books.

1983—Creates Parachute Press with wife Jane.

1984—Scholastic stops publishing *Bananas*. Scholastic publishes Stine's first horror book, *Horrors of the Haunted Museum*.

1984–1985—Becomes editor of Scholastic's *Maniac* magazine. Takes on a variety of freelance writing jobs, including bubble gum cards for the *Zero Heroes* card series, *Indiana Jones*, and *James Bond* "Find-Your-Fate" books, *G I Joe* adventure stories, Mighty Mouse and Bullwinkle coloring books, many joke books such as *101 Silly Monster Jokes* and *Sick of Being Sick*, and the *Madball* series. Also takes on the job of head writer for Nickelodeon's *Eureka's Castle*.

1985—Is approached by Scholastic editor Jean Feiwel to write a horror book called *Blind Date*. Leaves Scholastic as editor of *Maniac* magazine.

1986—*Blind Date*, Stine's first horror novel for young adults, is published by Scholastic. The book becomes an instant best-seller.

1987—Publishes his second horror novel for young adults, *Twisted*. It becomes a best-seller.

1989—Publishes his third horror novel for young adults, *The Baby-Sitter*. It becomes a best-seller. This is followed by *The New Girl*. They become the first of four *Baby-Sitter* books and the *Fear Street* series is conceived.

1990—Publishes two funny novels with Archway Paperbacks, *Phone Calls* and *How I Broke Up With Ernie*.

1991—Publishes his first *Fear Street Super Chiller*, called *Party Summer*. The idea for *Goosebumps* is conceived.

1992—Scholastic publishes Stine's first *Goosebumps* novel, *Welcome to the Dead House*. This is followed by *Monster Blood*, and the first *Fear Street* trilogy, *Cheerleaders*.

1993—Publishes the *Fear Street Saga* trilogy.

1994—The popularity of *Goosebumps* sweeps the country. Stine takes over *USA Today*'s best-seller list.

1995—Publishes his first adult novel, *Superstitious*, with Warner Books. *Goosebumps* weekly TV show begins with a Halloween special featuring "The Haunted Mask." Stine works as an adviser for the series. *People* magazine hails Stine as one of the most interesting people of the year. Controversy about Stine's work appears in an article in *The Weekly Standard*. Stine continues to be named #1 by *USA Today* as the best-selling author in America.

1996—*Fear Street Sagas* and *Goosebumps Presents* are launched. *Goosebumps* becomes available as a CD-ROM. *Goosebumps* products hit the marketplace. For the third year in a row, Stine holds the *USA Today* title as best-selling author in the country. Stine and his family move into a larger apartment on Manhattan's Upper West Side.

1997—Stine and college friend Joe Arthur write Stine's autobiography, *It Came From Ohio! My Life as a Writer*, published by Scholastic. *Goosebumps* sales falter. Disney-MGM Studios in Orlando, Florida, opens the Horrorland and Fun House attraction based on *Goosebumps*. Golden Books and Parachute Press join forces to publish sixty-five new *Fear Street* books. Stine agrees to do a *Goosebumps* movie with Fox Family Films. The controversy about Stine's books escalates.

1998—*Goosebumps 2000* series is published by Scholastic. Disney World opens a *Goosebumps* attraction.

1999—Parachute Press and HarperCollins publish *Nightmare Hour*, an anthology of ten of Stine's scariest original stories and the first hardcover trade book collection for children eight and older.

2000—*Guinness World Records Millennium Edition 2000* declares *Goosebumps*, with sales of 220 million copies, as the world's best-selling children's book series and Stine as the best-selling children's author. Stine's *The Nightmare Hour* is on the *New York Times* Best Seller List, Children's Listing. Parachute Publishing and HarperCollins Children's Books release *The Nightmare Room* series and the website www.thenightmareroom.com. *Locker 13* (*Nightmare Room* series), wins the *Disney Adventures'* Kid's Choice Awards as Best Horror/Mystery Book. Stine is chosen by students across America as their second favorite writer in the world (NEA).

2001—*The Nightmare Room* television series airs on the Kids' WB network. Stine is a guest at Governor Jeb Bush's "Celebration of Reading" in Florida.

2002—*Beware!: R. L. Stine Picks His Favorite Scary Stories* is published by HarperCollins.

2003—Publishes *Dangerous Girls*, the first book in the *Dangerous Girls* (*Fear Street*) series. Stine accompanies Laura Bush to Moscow and attends the Russian Book Festival. Stine and Ballantine Books publish Stine's second adult thriller, *The Sitter*.

2004—Stine, Random House/Delacorte Press, and Parachute Press introduce a new series of hardcovers called *Mostly Ghostly*. *Dangerous Girls* appears on the ALA's "Quick Picks" for Reluctant Young Adult Readers list.

SPOOKY STORIES
OF R. L. STINE

1989—*The Baby Sitter*
    The New Girl
    (Fear Street)
    The Overnight
    (Fear Street)
1990—*Beach Party*
    The Boyfriend
    Curtains
    Halloween Party
    (Fear Street)
    How I Broke Up with
    Ernie
    Missing (Fear Street)
    Phone Calls
    The Stepsister
    (Fear Street)
    The Surprise Party
    (Fear Street)
    The Wrong Number
    (Fear Street)
1991—*The Amazing*
    Adventures of Me,
    Myself and I
    The Baby Sitter II
    The Fire Game
    (Fear Street)
    The Girlfriend
    Haunted (Fear Street)
    Lights Out
    (Fear Street)

Party Summer (Fear
    Street Super Chillers)
The Secret Bedroom
    (Fear Street)
Silent Night (Fear
    Street Super Chillers)
Ski Weekend
    (Fear Street)
The Sleepwalker
    (Fear Street)
The Snowman
Son of Furry
1992—*Beach House*
    The Best friend
    (Fear Street)
    First Date
    (Fear Street)
    The First Evil (Fear
    Street Cheerleaders)
    Goodnight Kiss (Fear
    Street Super Chillers)
    Hit and Run
    The Knife (Fear Street)
    Monster Blood
    (Goosebumps)
    The Prom Queen
    (Fear Street)
    Say Cheese and Die!
    (Goosebumps)
    The Second Evil (Fear
    Street Cheerleaders)

*Stay Out of the
Basement
(Goosebumps)*
*The Third Evil (Fear
Street Cheerleaders)*
*Welcome to Dead
House (Goosebumps)*
1993—*Baby Sitter III*
*Be Careful What
You Wish For
(Goosebumps)*
*The Betrayal
(Fear Street Saga)*
*Broken Hearts (Fear
Street Super Chillers)*
*The Burning
(Fear Street Saga)*
*The Cheater
(Fear Street)*
*The Curse of the
Mummy's Tomb
(Goosebumps)*
The Dead Girlfriend
*Escape from the
Carnival of Horrors
(Give Yourself
Goosebumps)*
*The First Horror
(Fear Street: 99 Fear
Street)*
*The Ghost Next Door
(Goosebumps)*
*The Girl Who
Cried Monster
(Goosebumps)*
Halloween Night
*The Haunted Mask
(Goosebumps)*
Hitchhiker
*Let's Get Invisible
(Goosebumps)*

*Night of the
Living Dummy
(Goosebumps)*
*Piano Lessons
Can Be Murder
(Goosebumps)*
*The Secret
(Fear Street Saga)*
*The Silent Night II
(Fear Street Super
Chillers)*
Sunburn (Fear Street)
*Welcome to Camp
Nightmare
(Goosebumps)*
*The Werewolf of
Fever Swamp
(Goosebumps)*
You Can't Scare Me
1994—*Attack of the Mutant
(Goosebumps)*
*Bad Dreams
(Fear Street)*
*Bad Moonlight (Fear
Street Super Chillers)*
The Beast
Call Waiting
*The Cheerleaders: The
New Evil (Fear Street
Super Chillers)*
The Dare (Fear Street)
*Deep Trouble
(Goosebumps)*
*The Dead Lifeguard
(Fear Street Super
Chillers)*
*Double Date
(Fear Street)*
The First Horror
*Ghost Beach
(Goosebumps)*

Go Eat Worms!
(Goosebumps)
Halloween Night II
Horrors of the
Haunted Museum
(Goosebumps)
I Saw You Last Night!
The Mind Reader
(Fear Street)
Monster Blood II
(Goosebumps)
My Hairiest
Adventure
(Goosebumps)
The New Boy
(Fear Street)
One Day at
Horrorland
(Goosebumps)
One Evil Summer
(Fear Street)
Phantom of the
Auditorium
(Goosebumps)
Return of the Mummy
(Goosebumps)
The Scarecrow Walks
at Midnight
(Goosebumps)
The Second Horror
(Fear Street: 99 Fear
Street)
Tales to Give You
Goosebumps
The Third Horror
(Fear Street: 99 Fear
Street)
The Thrill Club
(Fear Street)
Why I'm Afraid of
Bees (Goosebumps)
1995—*The Abominable*
Snowman of

Pasadena
(Goosebumps)
The Attack of the
Aqua Apes (Ghosts
of Fear Street) [With
A. G. Cascone]
The Barking Ghost
(Goosebumps)
The Baby Sitter IV
Bad Moonlight
The Beast II
College Weekend
(Fear Street)
The Cuckoo Clock of
Doom (Goosebumps)
The Dark Secret
(Fear Street: The
Cataluna Chronicles)
Dead End
(Fear Street)
The Deadly Fire
(Fear Street: The
Cataluna Chronicles)
Evil Moon
(Fear Street: The
Cataluna Chronicles)
Final Grade
(Fear Street)
The Haunted Mask II
(Goosebumps)
The Headless Ghost
(Goosebumps)
Hide and Shriek
(Ghosts of Fear
Street) [With Emily
James]
The Horror at
Camp Jellyjam
(Goosebumps)
It Came from
Beneath the Sink
(Goosebumps)

Monster Blood III
(Goosebumps)
More Tales to Give
You Goosebumps
The New Year's Party
(Fear Street Super
Chillers)
A Night in Terror
Tower (Goosebumps)
The Night of the
Living Dummy II
(Goosebumps)
Nightmare in 3-D
(Ghosts of Fear
Street) [With Gloria
Hatrick]
Revenge of the
Lawn Gnomes
(Goosebumps)
A Shocker on Shock
Street (Goosebumps)
The Stepsister II
(Fear Street)
Superstitious
Switched (Fear Street)
Tick, Tock, You're
Dead! (Give Yourself
Goosebumps)
Trapped in Bat Wing
Hall (Give Yourself
Goosebumps)
Truth or Dare
(Fear Street)
Who's Been Sleeping
in My Grave?
(Ghosts of Fear
Street) [With
Stephen Roos]
Wrong Number II
(Fear Street)
1996—A New Fear
(Fear Street Saga)

Attack of the
Jack-O'-Lanterns
(Goosebumps)
[With Carol Ellis]
Bad Hare Day
(Goosebumps)
The Beast from the
East (Goosebumps)
Beware of the Purple
Peanut Butter
(Give Yourself
Goosebumps)
Body Switchers from
Outer Space
(Ghosts of Fear
Street) [With Nina
Kiriki Hoffman]
The Boy Next Door
(Fear Street)
The Boy Who Ate Fear
(Ghosts of Fear
Street) [With
Stephen Roos]
The Bugman Lives!
Calling All Creeps!
(Goosebumps) [With
Carla Jablonski]
The Confession
(Fear Street)
The Creepy Creations
of Professor Shock
(Give Yourself
Goosebumps)
The Curse of the
Creeping Coffin
(Give Yourself
Goosebumps)
The Deadly
Experiments of Dr.
Eeek (Give Yourself
Goosebumps)

*Deep in the Jungle of
Doom (Give Yourself
Goosebumps)*
*Diary of a
Mad Mummy
(Give Yourself
Goosebumps)*
*Don't Ever Get Sick at
Granny's (Ghosts of
Fear Street)* [With
Jahnna N. Malcolm]
*Egg Monster from
Mars (Goosebumps)*
*Eye of the
Fortuneteller (Ghosts
of Fear Street)* [With
A. G. Cascone]
The Face (Fear Street)
*The Fear Street Saga
Collector's Edition*
*The First Scream (Fear
Street: Fear Park)*
*Fright Christmas
(Ghosts of Fear
Street)* [With
Stephen Roos]
*Fright Knight (Ghosts
of Fear Street)* [With
Connie Laux]
*Ghost Camp
(Goosebumps)*
*Goodnight Kiss II
(Fear Street Super
Chillers)*
*House of Whispers
(Fear Street Sagas)*
*How I Got My
Shrunken Head
(Goosebumps)*
*How to Be a Vampire
(Ghosts of Fear
Street)* [With Katy
Hall]

*How to Kill a Monster
(Goosebumps)*
*The Last Scream (Fear
Street: Fear Park)*
*Legend of the Lost
Legend
(Goosebumps)*
*Loudest Scream (Fear
Street: Fear Park)*
*A New Fear
(Fear Street Sagas)*
*Night Games
(Fear Street)*
*Night In Werewolf
Woods (Give Yourself
Goosebumps)*
*The Night of the
Living Dummy III
(Goosebumps)*
*Night of the Werecat
(Ghosts of Fear
Street)* [With
Katherine Lance]
*The Ooze (Ghosts of
Fear Street)* [With
Stephen Roos]
*The Perfect Date
(Fear Street)*
*Revenge of the
Shadow People
(Ghosts of Fear
Street)* [With Jahnna
N. Malcolm]
*Say Cheese and Die,
Again! (Goosebumps)*
*Scream of the Evil
Genie (Give Yourself
Goosebumps)*
*The Knight in
Screaming Armor
(Give Yourself
Goosebumps)*

Secret Admirer
(Fear Street)

Silent Night III (Fear
Street Super Chillers)

Stay Away from the
Tree House (Ghosts
of Fear Street) [With
Lisa Eisenberg]

Under the Magician's
Spell (Give Yourself
Goosebumps)

Vampire Breath
(Goosebumps)

Welcome to the Wicked
Wax Museum
(Give Yourself
Goosebumps)

What Holly Heard
(Fear Street)

1997—All-Night Party
(Fear Street)

Attack of the Beastly
Babysitter
(Give Yourself
Goosebumps)

The Best Friend II
(Fear Street)

Beware the Snowman
(Goosebumps)

The Blob That
Ate Everyone
(Goosebumps)

Camp Fear Ghouls
(Ghosts of Fear
Street) [With Jahnna
N. Malcolm]

Cat (Fear Street)

Chicken Chicken
(Goosebumps)

Children of Fear

The Creature from
Club Lagoona
(Ghosts of Fear
Street) [With Gloria
Hatrick]

The Creepy Creations
of Professor Shock
(Give Yourself
Goosebumps)

The Curse of Camp
Cold Lake
(Goosebumps)

Daughters of Silence

Deep Trouble II
(Goosebumps)

Detention (Fear Street)

Don't Go to Sleep!
(Goosebumps)

Escape from Camp
Run-For-Your-Life
(Give Yourself
Goosebumps)

The Evil Lives! (Fear
Street Super Chillers)

Fear Hall: The
Beginning
(Fear Street)

Fear Hall: The
Conclusion
(Fear Street)

Field of Screams
(Ghosts of Fear
Street) [With P.
MacFearson]

Goodnight Kiss
Collector's Edition
(Fear Street)

Goosebumps Triple
Header: Three
Shocking Tales of
Terror (Goosebumps)

The Haunted School
(Goosebumps)

The Hidden Evil

*High Tide (Fear Street
Super Chillers)*

*House of a Thousand
Screams (Ghosts of
Fear Street)* [With P.
MacFearson]

*How I Learned to Fly
(Goosebumps)*

*I Live In Your
Basement
(Goosebumps)*

*It Came From Ohio!
My Life as a Writer*
[As told to Joe
Arthur]

*Into the Dark
(Fear Street)*

*Killer's Kiss
(Fear Street)*

*Little Comic Shop of
Horrors
(Give Yourself
Goosebumps)*

*Midnight Diary
(Fear Street)*

*Monster Blood IV
(Goosebumps)*

*More and More and
More Tales to Give
You Goosebumps*

*My Best Friend is
Invisible
(Goosebumps)*

*Please Don't Feed
the Vampire!
(Give Yourself
Goosebumps)*

*Return to the
Carnival of Horrors
(Give Yourself
Goosebumps)*

Rich Girl (Fear Street)

Runaway (Fear Street)

*Scream of the Evil
Grave (Give Yourself
Goosebumps)*

*Secret Agent Grandma
(Give Yourself
Goosebumps)*

*Shop Till You Drop . . .
Dead! (Give Yourself
Goosebumps)*

*Three Evil Wishes
(Ghosts of Fear
Street)* [With Carolyn
Crimi]

*Toy Terror: Batteries
Included
(Give Yourself
Goosebumps)*

*The Twisted Tale of
Tiki Island
(Give Yourself
Goosebumps)*

*Spell of the Screaming
Jokers (Ghosts of
Fear Street)* [With
Kathy Hall]

*Werewolf Skin
(Goosebumps)*

*Why I'm Not Afraid of
Ghosts (Ghosts of
Fear Street)* [With
Nina Kiriki
Hoffman]

*Who Killed the
Homecoming Queen?
(Fear Street)*

1998—*Are You Terrified Yet?
(Goosebumps 2000)*

*Alone in Snakebite
Canyon*

*Bride of the Living
Dummy
(Goosebumps 2000)*

It Came from the
Internet
Jekyll and Heidi
(Goosebumps 2000)
The Mummy Walks
(Goosebumps 2000)
Nightmare Hour
Revenge of the Body
Squeezers (Give
Yourself Goosebumps
Special Edition)
Return to Ghost Camp
(Goosebumps 2000)
Return to Horrorland
(Goosebumps 2000)
Scary Birthday to You!
Scream School
(Goosebumps 2000)
Ship of Ghouls
Slappy's Nightmare
(Goosebumps 2000)
Trick or . . . Trapped
(Give Yourself
Goosebumps Special
Edition)
Weekend at Poison
Lake (Give Yourself
Goosebumps Special
Edition)
The Werewolf in the
Living Room
(Goosebumps 2000)
Zombie School

2000—All-Day Nightmare
Danger Time
Dear Diary, I'm Dead
(Nightmare Room)
Don't Forget Me!
(Nightmare Room)
Ghost in the Mirror
(Goosebumps 2000)

Liar, Liar
(Nightmare Room)
Locker 13
(Nightmare Room)
My Name is Evil
(Nightmare Room)

2001—Shadow Girl
(Nightmare Room)
Camp Nowhere
(Nightmare Room)
The Howler
(Nightmare Room)
They Call Me Creature
(Nightmare Room)
The Haunting Hour
When Good Ghouls
Go Bad
Visitors
(Nightmare Room)

2002—Beware! R. L. Stine
Picks His Favorite
Scary Stories

2003—Dangerous Girls
The Sitter
Haunted Lighthouse

2004—Eye Candy
Have You Met My
Ghoulfriend?
(Mostly Ghostly)
Dangerous Girls # 2:
The Taste of Night
Who Let the
Ghosts Out?
(Mostly Ghostly)

2005—Little Camp of Horrors
(Mostly Ghostly)
One Night in
Doom House
(Mostly Ghostly)

CHAPTER NOTES

Chapter 1. Who Is R. L. Stine?

1. Author interview with R. L. Stine, May 20, 2004.
2. Joel H. Cohen, *R. L. Stine* (San Diego: Lucent Books, Inc., 2000), p. 51.
3. Ibid., p. 36.
4. Ibid., p. 37.
5. Ibid., p. 38.
6. Patrick Jones, *What's So Scary About R. L. Stine?* (Lanham: Scarecrow Press, Inc., 1998), p. 150.
7. "The #1 Best-Selling Children's Book Series of All Time is Back by Popular Demand!" *PR Newswire Online Edition via ForRelease.com*, <http://www.forrelease.com/D2003073/nyth141.P1.07312003152249.25123.html> (New York, July 3/PRNewswire, Copyright 2003, issued 07/31/2003, 2:22 PM GMT).
8. Jones, p. 2.
9. *Guinness 2000 Book of Records Millennium Edition* (Guinness Records, 1999), p. 138.
10. *The Nightmare Room*, n.d., <http://www.harperchildrens.com/features/nightmare/bio.htm> (February 7, 2005).
11. Cohen, pp. 60–63.
12. Marc Silver, "Horrors! It's R. L. Stine!," *U.S. News & World Report*, October 23, 1995, pp. 95–96.
13. Jones, p. 143.

14. *The Nightmare Room*, n.d., <http://www. thenightmareroom.com/writing-program.htm> (February 7, 2005).

15. "R. L. Stine's Haunted Lighthouse," *BuschGardens. com*, n.d., <http://www.buschgardens.com/ buschgardens/fla/as_rlstine.aspx> (March 8, 2005).

16. R. L. Stine, as told to Joe Arthur, *It Came From Ohio! My Life as a Writer* (New York: Scholastic, 1997), p. 18.

17. Author interview with R. L. Stine, May 20, 2004.

Chapter 2. Dare or Scare?

1. R. L. Stine, as told to Joe Arthur, *It Came From Ohio! My Life as a Writer* (New York: Scholastic, 1997), p. 13.

2. Ibid., p. 2.

3. Ibid., p. 14.

4. Ibid., p. 12.

5. Ibid., p. 14.

6. Ibid., p. 16.

7. Ibid.

8. Ibid., p. 17.

Chapter 3. Humble Beginnings

1. Author interview with R. L. Stine, May 20, 2004.

2. Patrick Jones, *What's So Scary About R. L. Stine?* (Lanham: Scarecrow Press, Inc., 1998), p. 3.

3. R. L. Stine, as told to Joe Arthur, *It Came From Ohio! My Life as a Writer* (New York: Scholastic, 1997), pp. 2, 5.

4. Ibid., p. 5.

5. Ibid., p. 42.

6. Joel H. Cohen, *R. L. Stine* (San Diego: Lucent Books, Inc., 2000), p. 8.

7. Stine, *It Came From Ohio!*, p. 43.

8. Ibid.

9. Ibid.

Chapter 4. The One-Fingered Typist

1. R. L. Stine, as told to Joe Arthur, *It Came From Ohio! My Life as a Writer* (New York: Scholastic, 1997), p. 18.

2. Author interview with R. L. Stine, conducted on May 20, 2004.

3. Joel H. Cohen, *R. L. Stine* (San Diego: Lucent Books, Inc., 2000), p. 12.

4. Stine, *It Came From Ohio!*, p. 8.

5. Ibid., p. 18.

6. Ibid.

7. Ibid., p. 19.

8. Cohen, p. 12.

9. Ibid., p. 18.

10. Ibid.

11. Stine, *It Came From Ohio!*, p. 28.

12. Author interview with R. L. Stine, May 20, 2004.

13. Cohen, p. 18.

Chapter 5. Scared or Scary?

1. R. L. Stine, as told to Joe Arthur, *It Came From Ohio! My Life as a Writer* (New York: Scholastic, 1997), p. 10.

2. Ibid., p. 10.

3. Author interview with R. L. Stine, May 20, 2004.

4. Stine, *It Came From Ohio!*, p. 33.

5. Ibid., p. 35.

6. Ibid.

7. Ibid., p. 37.

8. Ibid., p. 34.

9. Ibid., p. 20.

10. Ibid., p. 24.
11. Ibid., p. 28.

Chapter 6. Fast Cars and Girls

1. R. L. Stine, as told to Joe Arthur, *It Came From Ohio! My Life as a Writer* (New York: Scholastic, 1997), p. 41.
2. Ibid., p. 39.
3. Ibid.
4. Ibid., p. 43.
5. Ibid.
6. Author interview with R. L. Stine, May 20, 2004.
7. Ibid.
8. Stine, *It Came From Ohio!*, p. 44.
9. Ibid., p. 48.

Chapter 7. The Scariest Job of All

1. "A Score of Stars, Artists, and Entertainers Who Called Ohio Home," Nancy Gilson, *The Columbus Dispatch*, (Dispatch Arts Reporter, October 17, 1999), Joel H. Cohen, *R. L. Stine* (San Diego: Lucent Books, Inc., 2000), p. 22.
2. Author interview with R. L. Stine, May 20, 2004.
3. Cohen, p. 22.
4. Ibid., p. 23.
5. Ibid., p. 24.
6. Ibid., p. 22.
7. Ibid., p. 25.
8. R. L. Stine, as told to Joe Arthur, *It Came From Ohio! My Life as a Writer* (New York: Scholastic, 1997), p. 62.
9. Author interview with R. L. Stine, May 20, 2004.
10. Stine, *It Came From Ohio!*, p. 64.
11. Cohen, p. 29.

12. Ibid.
13. Ibid., p. 30.

Chapter 8. Biting the Big Apple

1. Author interview with R. L. Stine, May 20, 2004.
2. Patrick Jones, *What's So Scary About R. L. Stine?* (Lanham: Scarecrow Press, Inc., 1998), p. 11.
3. Joel H. Cohen, *R. L. Stine* (San Diego: Lucent Books, Inc., 2000), p. 32.
4. Jones, p. 11.

Chapter 9. Bananas and a Hot Date

1. Joel H. Cohen, *R. L. Stine* (San Diego: Lucent Books, Inc., 2000), p. 34.
2. R. L. Stine, as told to Joe Arthur, *It Came From Ohio! My Life as a Writer* (New York: Scholastic, 1997), p. 82.
3. Ibid., p. 83.
4. Ibid.
5. Ibid., p. 84.
6. Author interview with R. L. Stine, May 20, 2004.
7. Cohen, p. 35.
8. R. L. Stine, as told to Joe Arthur, *It Came From Ohio! My Life as a Writer* (New York: Scholastic, 1997), pp. 93–94.
9. Patrick Jones, *What's So Scary About R. L. Stine?* (Lanham: Scarecrow Press, Inc., 1998), p. 14.
10. Author interview with R. L. Stine, May 20, 2004.
11. Jones, pp. 38–39.
12. Author interview with R. L. Stine, May 20, 2004.
13. Ibid.
14. Stine, *It Came From Ohio!*, p. 96.
15. Author interview with R. L. Stine, May 20, 2004.
16. Stine, *It Came From Ohio!*, p. 97.

17. Author interview with R. L. Stine, May 20, 2004.

Chapter 10. Goosebumps and Ghosts

1. Author interview with R. L. Stine, May 20, 2004.
2. Ibid.
3. Joel H. Cohen, *R. L. Stine* (San Diego: Lucent Books, Inc., 2000), p. 36.
4. Author interview with R. L. Stine, May 20, 2004.
5. Cohen, p. 37.
6. Author interview with R. L. Stine, May 20, 2004.
7. Ibid.
8. Cohen, p. 38.
9. R. L. Stine, as told to Joe Arthur, *It Came From Ohio! My Life as a Writer* (New York: Scholastic, 1997), pp. 112–113.
10. Author interview with R. L. Stine, May 20, 2004.
11. Ibid.
12. Ibid.
13. Ibid.
14. Ibid.
15. Ibid.
16. "Author: R. L. Stine," *Kidsreads.com*, n.d., <http://www.kidsreads.com/authors/au-stine-rl.asp> (January 29, 2005).
17. "The 100 Most Challenged Books of 1990–1999," *American Library Association*, n.d., <http://www.ala.org/oif/bannedbooksweek/bbwlinks/top100challenged.htm> (January 29, 2005).
18. "For Librarians," *American Library Association*, n.d., <http://www.ala.org/ala/oif/bannedbooksweek/bbwlinks/librarians.htm> (January 2, 2005).
19. Patrick Jones, *What's So Scary About R. L. Stine?* (Lanham: Scarecrow Press, Inc., 1998), p. 204.
20. Ibid., p. 205.

21. "Third Annual State of American Education Address." Richard Riley. *United States Department of Education* (St. Louis, Mo.: February 28, 1996), <http://www.ed.gov/Speeches/02-1996/speech.html> (January 29, 2005).
22. Jim Trelease, *The Read Aloud Handbook*, 5th ed (New York: Penguin, 2001), p. 183.
23. Jones, p. 211.
24. Author interview with R. L. Stine, May 20, 2004.
25. Ibid.
26. Ibid.
27. Ibid.
28. Ibid.
29. Ibid.
30. Ibid.
31. Ibid.
32. Ibid.

Chapter 11. Just a Regular Guy

1. Author interview with R. L. Stine, May 20, 2004.
2. *The Nightmare Room*, n.d., <http://www.thenightmareroom.com> (February 7, 2005).
3. Author interview with R. L. Stine, May 20, 2004.
4. "Gov. Bush, Family Support Reading Awareness Goal." David Plazas, *The News-Press*, January 25, 2001 <http://www.myflorida.com/myflorida/government/governorinitiatives/aplusplan/articles/su> (January 29, 2005).
5. "Laura Bush Promotes Reading in Russia," Kathy Ishizuka, *School Library Journal* available at Keep Media, November 1, 2003, <http://www.keepmedia.com> (January 29, 2005).
6. Author interview with R. L. Stine, May 20, 2004.
7. Ibid.
8. Ibid.

GLOSSARY

affluent—To possess in overflowing abundance; wealthy.

ancillary—Something supplemental or additional.

bar mitzvah—A Jewish ceremony that takes place on a boy's thirteenth birthday, celebrating his attainment of the age of religious responsibility.

coed—When males and females are taught together at a school. Short for co-educational.

conjecture—A supposition or proposition that is offered without testing or proof.

consternation—A state of frustration or dismay.

contemporaries—When two or more people are of the same age or have lived together during a common period of time.

demographic—A statistic profile group.

emigrate—To leave one's place of origin and move elsewhere.

facetious—Meant humorously and not seriously.

genre—A category of art, literature, or music.

humility—The state of being humble.

inimitable—When someone or something cannot be imitated.

insatiable—Unable to be satisfied.

jovial—Good-humored or fun-loving.

niche—Something for which a person or thing is best-suited.

occult—Relating to magic or supernatural.

paraphernalia—Someone's equipment or accessories.

parody—When someone or something is imitated to humorous effect.

satire—A literary work that ridicules human weakness or vice.

shenanigans—Playful or mischievous activities.

smitten—To be enamored with or feel affection for someone.

spoof—A light parody.

supernatural—Dealing with mysterious or magical forces.

wry—Cleverly or ironically humorous.

zeal—Possessing enthusiasm and eagerness.

FURTHER READING

Cohen, Joel H. *R. L. Stine*. San Diego: Lucent Books, Inc., 2000.

Jones, Patrick. *What's So Scary About R. L. Stine?* Lanham: Scarecrow Press, Inc., 1998.

Stine, R. L., as told to Joe Arthur. *It Came From Ohio! My Life as a Writer*. New York: Scholastic, 1997.

Wheeler, Jill C. *R. L. Stine*. Edina, Minn.: Abdo & Daughters, 1996.

Internet Addresses

The Nightmare Room
  http://www.thenightmareroom.com

R. L. Stine !!!
  http://www.scholastic.com/goosebumps/books/
  stine

R. L. Stine Bibliography
  http://www.fantasticfiction.co.uk/authors/R_L_
  Stine.htm

INDEX